D0464288

Date

Nov. 2008

Dear Dani Jo

thanks for
bringing God
back into my
Life

From your friend Sue
Miles

My favorite `p. 17`

I Prayed for You Today

© Audrey Jeanne Roberts, licensed by Suzanne Cruise

© 2003 Christian Art Gifts, RSA
            Christian Art Gifts Inc., IL, USA

Designed by Christian Art Gifts

Christian Art Gifts has made every effort to trace the ownership of all quotes and poems in this book. In the event of any question that may arise from the use of any quote or poem, we regret any error made and will be pleased to make the necessary correction in future editions of this book.

Scripture taken from the *Holy Bible*, New International Version®. NIV®. Copyright © 1973, 1978, 1984 by International Bible Society. Used by permission of Zondervan Publishing House. All rights reserved.

ISBN 1-86920-321-6

Printed in China

06 07 08 09 10 11 12 – 10 9 8 7 6 5 4

I Prayed for You Today

Written and illustrated by
Audrey Jeanne Roberts

christian
art gifts

Now to him who is able to do immeasurably more than all we ask or imagine, according to his power that is at work within us, to him be glory in the church and in Christ Jesus throughout all generations, for ever and ever! Amen.

~ *Ephesians 3:20-21*

Author's note

Having been immeasurably blessed by the prayers of faithful friends throughout the course of my life – I pray that these thoughts and prayers will also bless you.

If you wake up in the morning and you feel you cannot find the strength to get up and face the day – I hope you will pick up this little book and remember that someone loves you dearly and is praying for you. But even more importantly, that you will remember your Heavenly Father – the Creator of the Universe, the One that holds all things in the palm of His hand – loves you and has a plan for your life.

May you find comfort, peace, strength and encouragement in the Lord who delights to answer the prayers of His people.

Audrey Jeanne Roberts

5

Contents

For this reason, since the day we
heard about you, we have not stopped
praying for you and asking God to fill
you with the knowledge of his will through
all spiritual wisdom and understanding.
And we pray this in order that you may live
a life worthy of the Lord and may please
him in every way: bearing fruit in every
good work, growing in the knowledge of God.

~ Colossians 1:9-10

8

Dear friend,

*My heart was filled with compassion as
I thought of you today.*

*I wanted you to know that you are deeply loved –
by me, by those who share your life and most
importantly by the God who is powerful
enough to have created Heaven and Earth,
yet compassionate enough to reach down and
tenderly dry our tears.*

*I've been through many hard times in my life,
and in each of them the Lord has faithfully
seen me through and I know He loves you so
much that He longs to do the same for you.*

9

When I have been overwhelmed
by life's most challenging moments,
the most encouraging thing
that anyone has said to me was,
"I prayed for you today."

I prayed for you today

I said a prayer for you today
and know God must have heard.
I felt the answer in my heart,
although He spoke no word.
I didn't ask for wealth or fame –
I knew you wouldn't mind.
I asked Him to send treasures of
a far more lasting kind.
I asked that He'd be near you
at the start of each new day,
to grant you health and blessings
and friends to share your way.
I asked for happiness for you
in all things great and small,
but it was for His loving care
I prayed the most of all.

~ Author unknown

*Praise be to the God and Father
of our Lord Jesus Christ, who has
blessed us in the heavenly realms with
every spiritual blessing in Christ.*

~ *Ephesians 1:3*

12

God of blessings,

Fill my friend's heart with Your love. Fill it with so many blessings that they cannot be contained and they spill over, blessing everyone who shares her life.

Bless her with clarity of thought and effectiveness in all her plans. Please bless the work of her hands with success in this world, and great fruitfulness in Your kingdom to come.

Amen

Praise be to the God and
Father of our Lord Jesus
Christ, the Father of compassion
and the God of all comfort, who
comforts us in all our troubles,
so that we can comfort those in
any trouble with the comfort we
ourselves have received from God.

~ 2 Corinthians 1:3-4

God of comfort,

Speak words of comfort and peace to her in the quiet, alone places of her day. Give her that peace that passes all understanding and isn't based on things that we can see or touch or hear, but on the sure foundation of Your promises, Your character and Your power.

Open her eyes to perceive the needs of others so that she can bring the comfort of the love she has received from You to those who are in need.

Amen

*Surely there is something in
the unruffled calm of nature that
overawes our little anxieties and
doubts: the sight of the deep-blue sky,
and the cluster of stars above,
seems to impart quiet to the mind.*

~ *Jonathan Edwards*

16

Lord of peace,

Let your peace surround her like a soft woven blanket on a cold winter's night.

When she feels confused and in pain, remind her that You have compassion. That You always come alongside Your children, walking with them through every difficulty – especially those they feel are too great to overcome.

Remind her that You will not allow her to suffer a burden too great to be borne and You will not allow her to bear it alone – for as You promised, You will never leave or forsake her.

Amen

Nearer my God, to Thee –
Nearer to Thee –
E'en though it be a cross
That raiseth me;
Still all my song shall be
Nearer my God, to Thee,
Nearer to Thee!

~ Sarah Flower Adams

18

Revealing God,

Reveal Yourself to my dear friend a little more each day. Show her the wonders of Your character and nature, the perfection of Your ways and the height and breadth and depth of the love You bear for her.

I pray that You would become even more real to her than I am! That she would come to recognize Your voice in the same way we recognize a loved one's greeting over the phone with just a simple "Hello!"

Amen

*You will be blessed in the city and blessed
in the country. You will be blessed when you
come in and blessed when you go out. The L*ORD
*will send a blessing on your barns and on everything
you put your hand to. The L*ORD *your God will
bless you in the land he is giving you. The L*ORD
*will establish you as his holy people, as he promised
you on oath, if you keep the commands of the L*ORD
*your God and walk in his ways. The L*ORD *will grant
you abundant prosperity – in the fruit of your womb,
the young of your livestock and the crops of your ground –
in the land he swore to your forefathers to give you.
The L*ORD *will open the heavens, the storehouse of
his bounty, to send rain on your land in season and
to bless all the work of your hands. You will lend*

to many nations but will borrow from none.
The LORD will make you the head, not the tail.
If you pay attention to the commands of the LORD
your God that I give you this day and carefully follow
them, you will always be at the top, never at the bottom.

~ *Deuteronomy 28:3,6,8-9,11-13*

God of love,

Speak to her daily of Your love for her and Your plans for her life.

When she reads Your Word, cause the words to spring to life. Teach her everything she needs to lead a blessed and godly life.

Give her the Christlike ability to love the un-lovely and even to love those that mistreat her. Let Your love, flowing in and through her, triumph over all.

Amen

And I pray that you,
being rooted and established in love,
may have power, together with
all the saints, to grasp how wide
and long and high and deep
is the love of Christ.

~ Ephesians 3:17-18

God of wisdom,

Fill her heart with wisdom. Cause her to grow in that wisdom each time she reads Your Word and applies it to her daily life.

Help her to see each aspect of life from the vantage point of Your throne and to daily seek Your wisdom and understanding for every challenge she faces.

Amen

But the wisdom that comes from heaven is first of all pure; then peace-loving, considerate, submissive, full of mercy and good fruit, impartial and sincere.

~ James 3:17

Faithful God,

As my friend grows to trust You more and more as she grows in the knowledge of You and Your faithfulness and goodness, gently mold her character until everyone around her notices how much she looks "just like her daddy!"

I pray that You would flood with the light of simple childlike faith any hiding place where doubt or discouragement is lurking, cloaked in darkness.

Amen

For this very reason,

make every effort to add

to your faith goodness;

and to goodness, knowledge.

~ 2 Peter 1:5

God of hope,

I pray that You would renew her hope and even give her new things to hope for.

If she's forgotten in the darkness what You've shown her in the light, refresh her vision and remind her of Your unfailing promises.

Amen

Far away in the sunshine are my highest aspirations. I may not reach them, but I can look up and see their beauty, believe in them, and try to follow where they lead.

~ Louisa May Alcott

Guiding God,

If my friend is wondering, "Am I on the right path?" I pray that You might allow her to see a little "sign post" that assures her she's still traveling in the right direction. Then put a song in her heart so the journey will seem to fly by!

Whisper in her ear a little about where You are taking her and help her to enjoy the daily journey instead of growing anxious to know "When will we be there?"

Amen

The heights of Christian perfection can only be reached by faithfully each moment following the Guide who is to lead you there, and He reveals your way one step at a time, in the little things of your daily lives, asking only on your part that you yield yourself up to His guidance.

~ Hannah Whitall Smith

God of miracles,

Bring some wonderful and unexpected miracle to her today. Arrange some delightful encounter that brings a smile to her face and a lightness to her step.

May your miracle-answers be in direct proportion to the depth of her need and may those skeptics who are observing her life, see in them the unmistakable fingerprints of Your hand of power!

Amen

Every moment of this strange and lovely life, from dawn to dusk, is a miracle.

~ Beverley Nichols

May the God of all blessings

fill your heart with joy today.

*You have made known to me
the path of life; you will fill me
with joy in your presence, with
eternal pleasures at your right hand.*

~ *Psalm 16:11*

36

God of joy,

If her experience of joy seems to have dimmed, I pray that You would renew it today and flood her with inexplicable, non-circumstantial, completely supernatural joy!

Give her joy in being loved by You. Joy in the wonder of your creation. Joy in the knowledge that You have a plan for her life – even if she can't see it for the moment.

Amen

Those who hope in the Lord
will renew their strength.
They will soar on wings like eagles;
they will run and not grow weary,
they will walk and not be faint.

~ Isaiah 40:31

Mighty God,

Give her strength to continue standing in faith, believing in Your Word and Your ways. Strengthen her character to choose the right course of action no matter how difficult it may seem.

Give her strength equal to the needs of this day. When she is weak and weary, give her physical strength that doesn't run out until the day does!

Amen

"Be still, and know
that I am God."

~ Psalm 46:10

Lord of the storm,

If unexpected events bring stormy seas and trouble the once-still waters of her life, give her the emotional strength and stability to calmly overcome them.

Remind her that You have power over every storm and You do not leave her to face them alone. Help her to be so at peace, resting by Your side, that just like You, she can sleep through even the heaviest seas!

Amen

"Because he loves me," says the Lord, "I will rescue him; I will protect him, for he acknowledges my name. He will call upon me, and I will answer him; I will be with him in trouble, I will deliver him and honor him. With long life will I satisfy him and show him my salvation."

~ Psalm 91:14-16

God of protection,

When her battles are spiritual, give her endurance, perseverance and spiritual power to continue to resist evil and cling to the good. Lord, develop her discernment so that she can easily distinguish between them.

Protect her from every plan of destruction that the enemy would launch. In fact, bring double-fold good for every evil attack. Cause the enemy to be defeated by his own plans and even come to regret the day he thought to send them her way!

Amen

Just for today I will try to adjust myself
to what is, and not try to adjust everything
to my own desires. Just for today I will be
unafraid, especially I will not be afraid
to be happy, to enjoy what is beautiful, to
love, and to believe that those I love, love me.

~ Sybyl Partridge

God of courage,

Give her wisdom for every situation she is facing, understanding to know how to act upon your wisdom and courage to continue walking wisdom's path all the way to the end – especially when she's growing weary or discouraged.

Lord, I ask that every need she has be met richly, exceedingly and abundantly by You – just as You have promised.

Amen

Would you know the blessing of all blessings? It is the God of Love dwelling in your soul. For all wants are satisfied ... every day is a day of peace ... because everything you see or do is all done in the sweet, gentle element of Love.

~ William Law

God of provision,

Wherever there is lack – bring plenty. Wherever there is plenty – show her wonderful ways to share it with others.

Yet, in plenty and in want, let her heart always rejoice with gratefulness for Your love and delight in Your goodness.

Amen